REA

FRIEN

OF ACPL

P9-CEP-055

362. K91

KROLOFF, CHARLES A.
54 WAYS YOU CAN HELP THE
HOMELESS

DO NOT REMOVE
CARDS FROM POCKET

ALLEN COUNTY PUBLIC LIBRARY
FORT WAYNE, INDIANA 46802

You may return this book to any agency, branch,
or bookmobile of the Allen County Public Library.

DEMCO

54 WAYS YOU CAN HELP THE HOMELESS

By Rabbi Charles A. Kroloff

Published by
Hugh Lauter Levin Associates, Inc. and
Behrman House, Inc.

Distributed by
Macmillan Publishing Company

Allen County Public Library
900 Webster Street
PO Box 2270
Fort Wayne, IN 46801-2270

©1993 Hugh Lauter Levin Associates, Inc. and Behrman House, Inc.

NOTE:
Fifty-four represents a multiple of the number 18,
which in the Jewish tradition represents "life."

You may reproduce this book entirely, or any section of it, for non-profit
use without seeking permission from the author or publisher provided
proper credit is given. This permission is granted in order to permit the
widest possible distribution of its contents in schools, religious institutions,
and by individuals who want to inform others about ways to help homeless
people.

Additional copies of the book can be ordered from the publisher.

All profits from the sale of this book will be donated to organizations that
are serving the homeless people of our nation. —*The Publishers*

Behrman House Inc.   Hugh Lauter Levin Associates, Inc.
235 Watchung Ave.   2507 Post Rd.
West Orange, NJ 07052   Southport, CT 06490
Adam Bengal, Managing Editor

ISBN 0–88363–888–6
Printed in the United States of America

TABLE OF CONTENTS

INTRODUCTION

Rabbi Charles A. Kroloff

I have never been homeless. But I often wondered what it would be like to live, night after night, on the streets or in a public shelter.

I have, however, spent long restless evenings sleeping with homeless men, women, and children at our Temple's shelter (a school by day). Time after time, I found myself waking, flooded by the sadness that decent people were sleeping in our classrooms, all their remaining possessions crammed into shopping bags.

The world of the homeless is very far from mine—but in some ways it is quite near. For any of us, the loss of a job, the death of a spouse or a child, a severe physical disability, family problems, could be the route to total despair. These are the very tragedies that have happened to many homeless people. Struck by personal tragedies, the people in our shelter and in thousands of others across America, have lost their homes and been deserted by the families and friends they once had.

But we have another choice: to be strengthened. Like any other problem, we can choose whether we will allow ourselves to be defeated by it or if we will emerge stronger for seeking solutions and offering a helping hand.

This is the time we ask, "What can I do?"

This is the time we tap our hidden resources and strengths.

This is the time we turn to other people, to the community, to religion for strength, guidance, and assistance.

If you have never witnessed the despair of the homeless first hand, it is easier to ignore them, and abandon them. Even to assume that homeless people are all derelicts, mentally ill, drug addicts — people beyond help, people who don't deserve assistance.

As you will learn in this book, there are miracles that have been accomplished for displaced people — and by homeless people who are able to put their broken lives back together. I marvel at the resiliency and the potential we all have, including the hundreds of thousands who will spend tonight in a shelter, on the streets, or living in an abandoned car.

What can you do, personally, to help them? Sometimes the smallest gesture—and a good attitude—can go a long way. You can start by reading on.

I

Learn About The Homeless

3 1833 02265 1407

UNDERSTAND WHO THE HOMELESS ARE 1

The first—and most important—thing you can do to help the homeless is to realize that the tired old stereotypes concerning them just are not true.

Myth: They want to be homeless.
Fact: Less than six percent of the homeless are that way by choice.

Myth: They're to blame for being homeless.
Fact: Most homeless are victims. Some have suffered from child abuse or violence. Nearly one quarter are children. Many have lost their jobs. All have lost their homes.

Myth: They don't work.
Fact: Many homeless people are among the working poor. A person earning minimum wage can't earn enough to support a family of three or pay inner-city rent.

Myth: They are mentally ill.
Fact: About 25 percent of the homeless are estimated to be emotionally disturbed. One percent may need long-term hospitalization; the others can become self-sufficient with help.

Myth: They are heavy drug users.
Fact: Some homeless are substance abusers: research suggests one in four. Many of these are included in the 25 percent who suffer from mental illness.

Myth: They are dangerous.
Fact: Sometimes an encounter with the homeless may end in tragedy. It is extremely rare, though. In general, the homeless are among the least threatening group in our society. If anything, they are the victims of crimes, not the perpetrators.

Most homeless people are not drunks or drug abusers or former mental patients. Most are able or willing to work. They are not the perpetual social problem many people believe they are. So who are they?

Full-time workers

One out of four homeless is employed full- or part-time, according to the United States Conference of Mayors. The arithmetic is simple and frightening: a person who works forty hours a week at the 1992 Federal minimum wage of $4.25 per hour grosses about $700 a month, takes home less than $600—and is a prime candidate for homelessness.

I meet such people at a shelter run by my synagogue in Westfield, New Jersey. Two neatly dressed sisters in their thirties arrived one evening. One was a full-time sales clerk at Bloomingdale's; her sister was seeking a job. Two rent increases in a year had eaten their savings and caused them to fall behind in rent. Consequently, they were evicted. By using the Temple's hospitality program, they hoped to save enough for first and last months' rent and a security deposit for an apartment.

Disabled vets

One quarter of the homeless are war veterans, most of them from the Vietnam conflict. Do you remember Ron Kovic's story in the film, *Born on The Fourth of July*? It dramatized the fact that the veterans of that war were abandoned and discouraged, even dishonored, and in Ron's case, wound up on our streets, some of them disabled, others mentally traumatized by their war experiences, others simply unable to find work.

Children

One out of four homeless people is a child. The fastest growing homeless group in the United States is families with children. Their number nearly doubled between 1984 and 1989, and continues to do so.

Even more appalling, many homeless children are alone. They may be runaways who left home because there is no money for food, because they are victims of rape, incest, or violence or because one or both of their parents is in emotional turmoil. Some are "throwaways" whose parents tell them to leave home, or won't allow them to return once they leave.

I was shocked to learn that in Washington, D.C. , when a

soup kitchen, Martha's Kitchen, was opened to serve destitute children, within three weeks they were serving thirty children a day.

The Elderly

Elderly people on fixed incomes don't fit the traditional image of homeless folk. But the fact is that a senior citizen who receives $450 a month in benefits and pays $350 for rent can't survive in any U.S. city. However, Social Security, Medicare, and other senior-oriented programs provide a safety net for many of the elderly, making their numbers disproportionally less among the homeless than other minorities. Although the elderly are not as likely to be found in shelters, it is true that some are afraid to go to shelters, or even a soup kitchen. Others are living in poverty, not homeless, but often homebound and without proper heating, water, or other amenities.

AIDS victims

Thirty-two thousand people with AIDS and their dependents were homeless in 1989. By 1995 over 100,000 AIDS-related sufferers are projected to join their ranks.

Fast facts

*The number who are homeless for at least one night during the year is probably over three million.

*The majority of homeless are male; the largest proportion are single men.

*Illegal immigrants are swelling the ranks of the homeless.

*One child in five lives below the poverty line, making children the poorest age group in the United States, which accounts for the growing percentage of children who are homeless.

*Many homeless people have completed high school; some have attended college and even graduate school.

*The homeless are found not only in cities, but in small towns, rural areas, and affluent suburbs.

*Millions are among the hidden homeless—people who are one crisis away from losing their homes. They may be doubled or tripled up in housing or 48 hours from eviction or about to leave a hospital with nowhere to go.

2 EDUCATE YOURSELF ABOUT THE HOMELESS

You've already taken your first step by reading this book. You've discovered that the homeless are more than the stereotypical drifter, drunk, or bum. A homeless person may be someone with a job, a runaway kid, a member of your family. Or you yourself.

You may already know the homeless in your community by sight. You may have spoken to them and know their names. Or you might have never noticed them at all. One of the first steps in helping people is to see them as individuals and to find out what they need.

Notice them; talk to them. Most are starved for attention. And contact your local religious centers, social service agencies, or town hall to find the programs in your community that aid the homeless. (Many national organizations are listed in the back of this book.)

Don't be afraid to reach out—or to pass along what you have learned to others. You can start by sharing this book with a friend.

❋

Public opinion polls reveal that American people consider homelessness a top priority and are willing to pay more taxes to solve the problem. Americans are mostly a compassionate people, and we are troubled by the enormous gaps between rich and poor in our land. Many of us do not sleep easily knowing that hundreds of thousands of men, women, and children are sleeping on grates, under bridges, and in doorways. Many of us do not enjoy our meals knowing that vast numbers of Americans are going hungry.

RESPECT THE HOMELESS AS INDIVIDUALS 3

What we are willing to do for homeless people is to a large extent a matter of our attitude toward them. If you think that they are human debris, if you assume that they will always be living in the street and in shelters, you probably also believe that any help you might give would be a wasted effort. At worst, some people firmly believe that any help given only encourages indigence.

But what if we believe that, like the rest of us, they have untapped resources? True, sometimes their potential seems to be unreachable. Their talents, buried deep within, are covered by layers of neglect, self-abuse, or illness.

With patience, you can tap those resources. The first step is to give the homeless people the same courtesy and respect you would accord your friends, your family, your employer. Treat them as you would wish to be treated if you needed assistance.

Gerald Winterlin's plunge into homelessness began when he was laid off in May 1982, and he was unable to find another job. He soon lost his home and slept in the rear of his station wagon. When that broke down, he spent nights in abandoned homes.

A program which aided dislocated workers encouraged him to take a skills test. With the help of a federal Pell grant for low-income people, he enrolled in junior college. His academic record was rewarded by a scholarship at the University of Iowa. At 44, he graduated with a degree in accounting and a grade point average of 3.966! He is currently employed as an accountant.

"There are a million Jerry Winterlins running around this country," he told me. Perhaps there are a million. Or maybe only 100,000. But vast numbers of homeless men and women who are capable of gaining their high school equivalency degree, attending college and holding down a productive job do exist. They need the chance.

4 BUY THIS BOOK

When you buy this book, you not only get suggestions for aiding the homeless, you're making a donation to a worthy cause. Proceeds from the sale of this book will be given to organizations that help the homeless.

Encourage your friends and family to get their own copies as well. You may wish to purchase extras to donate to your local church or synagogue or other community organizations. The more people who are aware of the homelessness problem and what they can do to help, the more homeless people will be helped.

After reading the galley proofs of this book, my sister in Maryland resolved to do something to help the homeless. Within three days, she was helping out at a soup kitchen.

A church educator who also saw proofs ordered a copy for every ninth and tenth grader in her Sunday School.

Someone who heard about the gift certificates for fast-food restaurants (see page 21) went out and purchased a supply of vouchers for the homeless.

By distributing this book nationally, and by making it possible for anyone to reproduce the contents without permission, it is our hope that thousands of others will have the same reactions as those who have read it before publication — to extend themselves to help the homeless, and to multiply the number of copies available.

If you cannot find copies in your bookstore, you will find instructions on how to order copies in the front of this book.

II

What To Do When Confronted By The Homeless

RESPOND WITH KINDNESS 5

You are walking down the street of your town when someone approaches you for coffee, a meal, or a bus ticket to a town where "there are relatives who will help."

How do you respond?

I conducted an informal study, asking friends and relatives what they think at that moment:

"She needs it more than I."

"Hey, fella, McDonald's is hiring."

"My heart says, 'Give,' but my head says, 'Don't be a fool.'"

"I've already given five bucks this week. It's starting to affect my budget."

"I help in other ways. I work at a shelter, support social agencies, and pay taxes."

The world of the homeless is confusing. Not only do professionals and volunteers involved with the homeless wrestle with difficult questions such as this—so does the average person who is approached on a subway platform, or while walking down the street minding his or her own business.

Amazingly, we can make quite a difference in the lives of the homeless when we respond to them, rather than ignore or dismiss them. Try a kind word. Remember, their self-confidence is nearly non-existent. Whatever we can say or do that gives them even an iota of self-worth will have some benefit.

The actor Danny Aiello never passes a person on the street without giving something. If he has no money he at least gives them a kind word. He never yells at them or says, "Get a job."

Every day a blind homeless man recognizes Aiello by his aftershave.

*He says "Hi, Danny" and "Thanks." He hears no coins hitting his
plate. Danny always gives him a bill.*

*Phyllis Cohen still remembers the homeless woman she encountered at
New York's Penn Station. She gave the woman $1 and asked her
which was the nearest exit to Macy's.*

*"Her face lit up like a corpse come to life," Ms. Cohen recalls. "She
gave me detailed directions and walked with me to be sure I got it
right, talking animatedly all the way. It seemed as though by asking
something of her, by assuming she had something to give, I had
validated, or reinstated, her personhood.*

*"I think of her often, of her reacting as though I'd given her a great
gift. Sometimes I consider going to Penn Station to seek her out, but I
hope not to find her there."*

CARRY FAST-FOOD GIFT CERTIFICATES 6

We've all been panhandled for change to buy a cup of coffee or get a bite to eat. If you're like most, you've been suspicious from time to time, wondering what the money was really for.

That's why my daughter's friend carries fast-food gift certificates. When he's approached for spare change, he hands out a certificate and points the way to the nearest Burger King or McDonald's. In this way, he doesn't ignore someone who's in need, but he knows his funds are used for food.

❋

Suspicion is sometimes well-placed. We don't want to be taken advantage of. Recently I received a call from a man passing through town who needed money. "My shoes are worn out and my feet are starting to swell. Can you give me $50 for shoes?"

I'd grown tired of phone scams — the clergy are considered by many to be an easy touch.

"I can't give you cash," I told him, "but I will meet you at the shoe store and buy you a pair of shoes." Certain my caller wouldn't show, I made my way downtown. To my surprise he was there at the shoe store waiting for me — his severely deformed foot encased in a tattered shoe.

Since that day I've often thought: What if I allow my suspicions and apprehensions to get the best of me? What if all of us were to allow our distrust to shape our responses to the needy people who seek our help?

7 DEVELOP LISTS OF SHELTERS

A member of my congregation who works in downtown Newark, New Jersey, carries cards listing the names, addresses, and telephone numbers of three nearby shelters and feeding programs. He figures that if one in fifty of the homeless he sees heads for a shelter, he has done a good deed.

The Women's Club of New York City publishes an easy-to-use directory of shelters for homeless women. Consider issuing such a directory for your area.

To find shelters and transitional housing programs in your community, look in the Yellow Pages of your phone book under Social and Human Services or Volunteer Services. Or contact your local church, synagogue, or social service agencies.

Born in Chicago, James had come to Los Angeles to work as a nurse's assistant. But a broken foot that required surgery to insert two screws had left him disabled.

Fortunately he found the Pershing Hotel on LA's Skid Row — operated by All Saints' Church and the Leo Baeck Temple. The Pershing is the first of many old hotels on Skid Row that are being refurbished by the Skid Row Housing Trust, a remarkable investment group dedicated to making Skid Row a welcoming supportive place for the homeless.

Another resident, Brenda, offered to teach James how to sew—and how to cook in the hotel's kitchen. He looked forward to the lessons and to group visits to the Los Angeles Music Center. He planned to take the test for a post office job: the same work his parents had done. As James proudly showed me his room, I sensed that these surroundings would go a long way toward literally getting him back on his feet.

The image of men and women hanging out in shelters, waiting for their lives to run out, is shattered by the care and energy emanating from places like the Pershing Hotel.

BUY *STREET NEWS* 8

The opportunity to help can be as close as the street corner of any major American city. In March 1990, my daughter paused near Columbia University to purchase the latest copy of *Street News* from a homeless man. *Street News* is a biweekly newspaper that includes articles by celebrities, business executives, and the homeless and is intended to help the homeless help themselves.

When they ask, homeless people are given free starter kits of *Street News* by the publishers to hawk on streets and public areas. From the proceeds the homeless vendors earn, they can buy further copies of the paper for 25 cents each and sell them for a dollar. For every paper sold, the homeless earn five cents deposited in a special savings account earmarked for rent. The vendor at Columbia told my daughter, "I have been able to rent a room on what I made selling *Street News*."

The idea for Street News *came to Hutchinson Persons, founder and the paper's first editor, one day while walking through Grand Central Station. "What an untapped work force," he reports thinking. "All these people just lying around here. But what can they do? This thought plagued me off and on, day and night, for about a week until suddenly it hit me...they could sell papers."*

According to Persons, a thousand homeless and nearly homeless men and women sold more than one million copies in New York City alone in the first few months of publication. Distribution is expanding to other cities.

9 BRING FOOD

It's as simple as taking a few extra sandwiches when you go out. When you pass someone who asks for change, offer him or her something to eat. If you take a lunch, pack a little extra. When you eat at a restaurant, order something to take with you when you leave.

Living on the street means being hungry. Without money to buy meals, homeless street people are forced to rely on soup kitchens and whatever they can get from passersby or from rummaging through trash cans.

�֍

Karen Olsen's job brought her to New York once or twice a week. As she passed through the Port Authority Bus Terminal she could not ignore the growing numbers of homeless people there.

Unlike other commuters, Karen stopped to talk with them. She learned that they were hungry more often than not. She decided she could do something. Enlisting the help of her children, they made sandwiches at home, and on weekends went to the bus terminal to distribute them.

Among the homeless was a former English teacher whom Karen's twelve-year-old son befriended.

"How did this happen to you?" he asked.

"I had enough money for food or shelter, but not for both," she responded. Since shelter was available in public areas, she chose to spend what little she had on food. When the boy made his weekend visits, she helped tutor him in his English assignments.

Karen's son discovered that his unemployed part-time tutor was a professional educator very much in touch with the reality of being homeless and hungry. She was also ready and willing to use her skills to help the child who helped her.

Karen was inspired by this first experience with the homeless to establish an interfaith shelter program in her community, and has now become the director of the National Interfaith Hospitality Networks.

III

Give To The Homeless

GIVE MONEY 10

One of the most direct ways to aid the homeless is to give money. Donations to organized charities and social service agencies that serve the homeless go a long way. Here are a few suggestions:

—make a donation to an organization, church, or synagogue that helps the homeless. Do it in memory of a late family member or friend;

—if you are inviting guests to a birthday or anniversary celebration, suggest that instead of gifts they contribute to an agency that helps the homeless and hungry;

—"adopt" one charity and make regular or yearly donations;

—give to annual drives (United Way, local food drives, etc.);

—help support neighborhood programs to aid the homeless (shelters, soup kitchens, transitional housing, counseling services, etc.).

Teddy Gross, a playwright who lives on Manhattan's Upper West Side, was running in Riverside Park one day and looked up at all the buildings. "I saw in my mind this huge penny bank," he said. So he began knocking on neighbors' doors asking if they would give their unused pennies to help the homeless. By the time he had solicited his floor, he had a few hundred dollars. When he finished with his building and a few friends had gone through their buildings, several thousand dollars had been collected.

In its first year, Common Cents New York, Inc. organized five campaigns during which more than 400 people harvested the buildings where they lived. That paid for 50,000 meals prepared by soup kitchens, three weeks of summer camp for 71 homeless kids, a van for a shelter, hundreds of blankets, coats, and sets of thermal underwear, and recreational programs in family shelters. Every penny harvested goes to the homeless. Not one penny is used for expenses.

For information, contact Common Cents New York, Inc.

11 GIVE RECYCLABLES

In localities where there is a "bottle law," collecting recyclable cans and bottles is often the only "job" available to the homeless. But it is an honest job that requires initiative. You can help by saving your recyclable bottles, cans, and newspapers and giving them to the homeless instead of taking them to a recycling center or leaving them out for city or county collection.

If you live in a larger city, you may wish to leave your recyclables outside for the homeless to pick up—or give a bagful of cans to a homeless person in your neighborhood. In smaller communities, you can take your recyclables to a local shelter.

In 1983 the Returnable Container Act was enacted in New York, which required stores in the state to accept up to 240 reusable cans and bottles per day from any single collector. The collector received five cents per container.

But most of Manhattan's supermarkets—including A&P, D'Agostino's, and Food Emporium—would not take 240 cans. What does a homeless person who collects recyclables do when stores flaunt the law?

Enter Doug Lasdon, executive director of the Legal Action Center for the Homeless. Using New York University Law School volunteers and homeless collectors, his investigation revealed that ten stores would not take a single can and that the most any would take was sixty.

Lasdon brought a class action suit on behalf of the homeless and obtained an injunction. He won the suit, protecting the civil rights of homeless people to return cans and bottles just like you or me. Your recyclables, plus help from the Legal Action Center, open up another path of hope for the homeless.

GIVE PROCEEDS FROM A CRAFT SALE 12

Whatever your specialty or interest, chances are you can organize a sale around it to benefit organizations that aid the homeless. Ask friends and family with similar interests to donate their time and talent to the sale. Perhaps you enjoy cooking or baking. Maybe you are handy with needlework or woodworking.

If you haven't time to make goods, consider holding a garage sale. You probably have a number of knickknacks, books, clothing, and other items that you no longer need. Whatever you make from selling these items, donate to your local shelter or soup kitchen. Invite your friends and family to donate their old treasures to your sale, too.

Lucinda Yates is a Maine artist and costume jewelry designer. "I started making 'house pins' as a way to raise money and awareness for my local shelter," says Lucinda. "I still can't believe how much they've caught on."

She now employs over sixty people and often takes orders at the rate of 1,000 a day for her one-of-a-kind high gloss enamel pins. Since she began in 1988, over 500,000 house pins have been sold.

Lucinda sells the pins for $6 each to buyers who must sign a contract promising to resell each pin for $10 with the profit going to organizations that serve the homeless. The Interfaith Housing Network of Ambler, PA netted over $15,000 in just one year.

The pins, which depict colorful houses, come in sizes as small as a tie tack or as large as 3 inches by 3 inches.

The pins also have great public relations value. When volunteers wear them, people ask about them and sometimes offer to help sell them. To find out more, contact House Pins, Inc., 180 Second Street, South Portland, ME 04106, (207) 799-6116.

13 GIVE CLOTHING

Next time you do your spring or fall cleaning, keep an eye out for those clothes that you no longer wear. If these items are in good shape, gather them together and donate them to organizations that provide housing for the homeless. Most shelters need to have clothing on hand.

Anybody can give clothing: union members, church goers, kindergarten kids, and senior citizens. Most of us have closets that need to be cleaned out!

New clothing, particularly socks and underclothing can be purchased and donated to shelters. Besides, having something new to wear gives a psychological lift.

Another example — in New York City this last winter, there was a drive to collect warm coats for the homeless. And for many years, one enterprising citizen has launched a "One-Glove" collection — volunteers match up the gloves into pairs, and distribute them in shelters.

Dayspring provides emergency 24-hour shelter for 60 people per night in Indianapolis, Indiana along with support services designed to help the homeless obtain jobs and permanent housing.

Three tables of clothing are set up each day, sorted by size and gender. Guests in the shelter are welcome to pick up what they need. Others in the neighborhood who are in need are also free to take what they require.

Sometimes Dayspring will hear about young children who do not have warm clothes for school. Dayspring will seek them out and invite them to take what they need.

What you do not need is desperately needed by others.

GIVE A BAG OF GROCERIES 14

During the holidays, synagogues, churches, and mosques may have a food drive for the poor. Load up a bag full of nonperishable groceries, such as canned goods, to donate. Encourage your neighbors and friends to participate as well.

If your community church or temple doesn't have a food drive, organize one. Contact your local soup kitchens, shelters, and homeless benefit societies and ask what kind of food donations they would like. Give people in your congregation or community notice about the food drive and ask for volunteers to help you collect the food and take it to the agency of your choice.

A church in Birmingham, Alabama asked every parishioner to bring a bag of groceries to the service on Easter Sunday. They filled six vans and replenished the local food pantry (whose stocks were depleted) with enough staples for the next month.

Reform synagogues throughout America ask their members to bring groceries on Yom Kippur which is a fast day. Instead of consuming food themselves, they provide nourishment for the hungry. Each synagogue collects between 500 and 10,000 pounds of food on the Jewish Day of Atonement.

According to the Biblical prophet Isaiah, the best kind of fast is the one that "feeds the hungry and lets the oppressed go free."

Many churches, mosques, and synagogues keep baskets in the lobby outside their sanctuary so members may deposit food for the hungry every day of the year. Homeless people don't just need sustenance by way of a Christmas or Thanksgiving feast . . . As the Lord's Prayer makes clear, "Give us this day our daily bread . . . "

15 GIVE TOYS

Children living in shelters have few possessions—if any—including toys. Homeless parents have more urgent demands on what little money they have, such as food and clothing. So, often these children have nothing to play with and little to occupy their time.

You can donate toys, books, and games to family shelters to distribute to homeless children. For Christmas or Chanukah, ask your friends and co-workers to buy and wrap gifts for homeless children. Donate them to organizations or programs that reach homeless children, such as Toys for Tots.

During one of my visits to a shelter, I arrived early and stood outside in the parking area watching four boys and girls as they careened around the lot on bicycles. Grinning from ear to ear, they were having the time of their lives.

Later I commented to the shelter's director on how much those kids were enjoying those bikes. She smiled knowingly and informed me that the bikes had just been dropped off the day before. A woman had discovered them in her basement. They had not been used for many years. Now they had new life and were giving much pleasure to kids who need to have fun.

GIVE
WELCOME KITS 16

Finding housing isn't the end of the matter for homeless people: usually they have no money or household items with which to furnish their new home. So they lack even the simplest necessities such as dishes, toilet paper, or towels.

To help them out, you can make "welcome kits" that include everyday basics such as cups, a pot and pan, soap, shampoo, toothbrushes, etc. Just think of the minimal items you would need to get by in a new home. Some things you may find around your own place; others you may get from friends. You could also approach local businesses about making contributions as well as local thrift shops, synagogues, or churches.

To distribute these "welcome kits," contact social services agencies or religious centers in your community with programs that find housing for homeless people.

A group of factory workers in St. Louis had been sitting at the same table in the company cafeteria eating lunch together every day for nearly 10 years. They obviously enjoyed each other's company. They complained about their problems and bragged about their accomplishments. It was a cozy group.

A few days before Thanksgiving, one of them suggested that since they had plenty of blessings—a good job, nice children, a car or van that ran well, decent health—maybe they should give something back to people who were very poor.

So they decided to put together "welcome kits," plastic bags consisting of toilet items, candy, and small items of clothing, like a hat, gloves, or socks. They all promised to bring a bag to lunch every Monday. Each week a different person would volunteer to take the bags to a local shelter.

17 GIVE A PORTION OF PARTY EXPENSES

MAZON, a Los Angeles-based national organization, encourages Jewish individuals and institutions to donate three percent of the cost of their bar mitzvahs, wedding celebrations, or group-sponsored meals. With more than 800 synagogues taking part, MAZON distributed $1.5 million to the hungry and homeless in 1992.

We can do the same if we all voluntarily taxed ourselves three percent of the total cost of our wedding, confirmation, bar or bat mitzvah or baptismal celebrations and gave this money to the homeless. Anyone who spends $1,000 for a party can surely afford another $30 for the needy. And it can be any party — not necessarily a ceremonial occasion — a birthday, a New Year's Eve, a Fourth of July picnic.

Such a gift sends a powerful message to our children and grandchildren.

I recall a couple preparing to celebrate their 40th wedding anniversary with two dozen family members. They discussed their options. Instead of an expensive restaurant meal, they chose a more modest home celebration. A check for the difference went to MAZON.

On another occasion, the father of a bride walked alongside me as we prepared to gather for a wedding processional. "Where should I send my three percent for MAZON?" he asked. As I approached the wedding canopy, I was inspired that some of us have heard the prophet Isaiah's admonition: to share our bread with the hungry and to bring the homeless into our midst.

GIVE THIS BOOK 18

You know that everyone's effort counts when it comes to a problem such as homelessness. Now you can spread the word to your friends, colleagues, and family by giving them this book. Instead of sending holiday cards this year, send people on your list a copy of this book. You'll be making a direct donation to causes helping the homeless as well as informing others of the problem homelessness has become and encouraging them to become involved.

Consider buying copies of this book and giving them to homeless people to sell. You would accomplish three things: the homeless would earn money, they would grow in self esteem, and more people would learn what they can do to help.

We repeat, one more reason to do it: the publishers' profits from this book go to agencies that help the homeless.

IV

Volunteer To Help The Homeless

VOLUNTEER AT A SHELTER 19

As you have already learned, there are many kinds of shelters — for battered women, for the elderly, for children, for drug addicts, for single mothers. As a volunteer, then, you have a wide choice.

Shelters thrive on the work of volunteers, from those who sign people in, to those who serve meals, to others who counsel the homeless on where to get social services. For the homeless, a shelter can be as little as a place to sleep out of the rain or as much as a step forward to self-sufficiency. A concerned volunteer can make a good deal of difference in their lives.

People who serve in shelters report that they have found it to be not only a spiritual moment, but also a time when their own burdens are lightened and their personal strength and courage are bolstered. I have personally felt a strong sense of God's presence at shelters, transitional housing, and wherever men, women, and children gather to feed, clothe, and protect those in need of all three.

I recall chairing a meeting in New York City attended by an Atlanta attorney who informed me that he intended to leave our session early to catch a mid-day flight back to Atlanta to serve meals at the shelter. "Chuck," he said in his Southern drawl, "I wouldn't miss that commitment for anything. Nothing I do is more important."

What is so significant about serving shelter meals that this attorney would shorten his trip? Could it be that with all of his success— financial, professional, personal—there remains an emptiness that does not let him rest? After all the vacations we take, the material goods we acquire, the honors we accumulate, do we sense that there is something else that we need to do to make our lives complete?

20 VOLUNTEER AT A SOUP KITCHEN

Soup kitchens provide one of the basics of life, nourishing meals for the homeless and other disadvantaged members of the community. Volunteers generally do much of the work, including picking up donations of food, preparing meals, serving it, and cleaning up afterward. To volunteer your services, contact your local soup kitchen, mobile food program, shelter, or religious center.

A teacher in Minnesota asked his class: "How many of you ate break-fast this morning?" As he expected, only a few raised their hands. So he continued, "How many of you skipped breakfast this morning because you don't like breakfast?" Lots of hands went up. "And how many of you skipped breakfast because you didn't have time for it?" Many other hands went up.

He was pretty sure by then why the remaining children hadn't eaten, but he didn't want to ask them about poverty, so he asked, "How many of you skipped breakfast today because your family just doesn't usually eat breakfast?" A few more hands were raised.

Then he noticed a small boy in the middle of the classroom, whose hand had not gone up. Thinking the boy hadn't understood, he asked, "And why didn't you eat breakfast this morning?" His face serious, the boy replied, "It wasn't my turn."

VOLUNTEER YOUR PROFESSIONAL TALENTS 21

No matter what you do for a living, you can help the homeless with your on-the-job talents and skills. Those with clerical skills can help nonprofit organizations and charities that reach the homeless. Doctors, psychiatrists, counselors, and dentists can treat the homeless in clinics. Lawyers can help with the legal concerns. The homeless' needs are bountiful—your time and talent won't be wasted.

The Rotary Clubs of the San Jose (CA) area sponsor Rotacare—free medical care for the homeless and others least able to afford it. Physicians and nurses see patients once a week in locations where the needy trust the caregivers—at soup kitchens, food pantries, clothing distribution centers, and shelters.

Rotacare was founded in 1988 by Dr. Mark Campbell who recognized that those who need medical care the most have the least access to it. Because time, space, and materials are mostly donated, Rotacare's budget is only $3,000 a year, primarily for insurance.

Two examples from Rotacare:

*One day a mother brought her son to see Dr. Campbell because the boy was doing poorly in school. On examining the child's ear, Dr. Campbell discovered a dead cockroach which had been there so long that it had destroyed the eardrum. He extracted the cockroach piece by piece and eventually arranged for an ear drum replacement.

*On another occasion, early one evening, nine children in one family residing at a shelter were checked for lice. Every child was infected. The last child asked Dr. Campbell to look at his mother. He found her outside the door, on the ground, sweating heavily. She had been suffering from chest pains since the morning. A paramedic team was called which saved her life.

This model can be used by other communities. Dr. Campbell would be pleased to provide information (408-866-8200).

22 VOLUNTEER YOUR HOBBIES

Every one of us has something we can give the homeless. Wherever our interests may lie—cooking, repairing, gardening, photography—we can use them for the homeless. Through our hobbies, we can teach them useful skills, introduce them to new avocations and perhaps point them in a new direction.

Volunteer your time at shelters or other organizations reaching the homeless—give demonstrations of what you do, teach classes or even just share your hobby one-on-one with a homeless person. Chances are, you'll reach many who are interested.

Take Jim Hubbard, a Washington, D.C. professional photographer whose specialty is photographing the homeless. Tapping his own skills, Hubbard created "Shooting Back," a program that teaches homeless children photography.

He takes eight homeless children each week through Washington's streets, provides them with free film and camera, and teaches them how to use the camera. The kids rarely shoot images of decay. "A lot of what they shoot is real joyful," stated Hubbard. "Kids leaping into swimming pools, playing in the water spray from fire hydrants, and the faces of other children."

When asked why he teaches children how to use a camera when what they need is shelter, Hubbard responded, "Housing won't be enough. Self-esteem is a big issue, particularly with children. Mastering the camera and seeing their own images in print have boosted their confidence."

VOLUNTEER FOR FOLLOW-UP PROGRAMS 23

A room, an apartment, or house is not enough unless there is also food, counseling, employment, medical care, and education. Some homeless people, particularly those who have been on the street for a while, may need help with fundamental tasks such as paying bills, balancing a household budget, or cleaning.

Follow-up programs to give the formerly homeless further advice, counseling, and other services need volunteers. Check with your local social service agencies, religious centers, and transitional housing groups to see what programs are in place and how your talents and skills can be used.

If nothing exists in your community, contact social services to find out what would be entailed in starting a program.

The Junior League of Plainfield (NJ) operates a "Casserole program" at the local center for the formerly homeless and others at risk of becoming homeless. Members prepare meals and bring them to the Wednesday lunch program where they share recipes with the guests and establish on-going relationships. They also bring food to the rooms or apartments of former guests.

Speakers come to the Wednesday lunch program and share their knowledge of parenting, AIDS education, legal rights, and medical information.

A retired professor at the local community college tutors five children in math and English once a week.

Three former guests at the center needed Christmas trees. Volunteers delivered them to their homes.

Do you have expertise in an area? Chances are you can share it through follow-up and make quite a difference in the lives of the needy as well as your own.

24 TUTOR HOMELESS CHILDREN

The stress of being homeless isn't something felt only by the adults of homeless families—the children reflect it, too. And it can affect their school performance. It's easy for these youngsters to fall behind their classmates in learning — often resulting in a decision to give up and drop out.

A tutor can make all the difference. Just having adult attention can spur children to do their best.

Many programs exist in shelters, transitional housing programs, and schools that require interested volunteers. Or begin your own tutor volunteer corps at your local shelter. It takes nothing more than a little time.

Megan Tingley is a children's book editor at Little Brown and Co. in Boston. Troubled by the large number of homeless—especially children—whom she encountered on Boston streets, she decided to do something to help them. Drawing on her own talents and experience, she created a small library at the Boston Family Shelter.

With the help of four co-workers and a grant from Time, Inc., Tingley reads stories aloud, has the children read to each other, and arranges for them to borrow the books. "Reading can empower young people and help them get a head start," she says.

TAKE HOMELESS CHILDREN ON TRIPS 25

Frequently, the only environment a homeless child knows is that of the street, shelters, or other transitory housing. Outside of school—if they attend—these children have little exposure to many of the simple pleasures that most kids have, such as going to the park or a zoo.

Taking them on trips gets them away from their situation and exposes them to new surroundings. Volunteer at your local family shelter to take children skating or to an aquarium on the weekend. Contact organizations such as the Children's Aid Society or your local shelter network to see what programs for homeless children they may have in which you can become involved. Join Big Brothers or Big Sisters and ask for a homeless child.

"Children First" was founded by the Interfaith Council for the Homeless of Union County, New Jersey to enhance homeless children's self-esteem through enrichment projects—individually and with their families through workshops and field trips.

On one field trip they visited the Morris Museum in Morristown (NJ), where youngsters and their parents viewed sunspots through a telescope and came face-to-face with a 12-foot boa constrictor. One of the goals is to teach parents how to participate in stimulating experiences with their children—in art and cooking workshops, puppet-making, and print-making.

26 BRING A MEAL TO THE HOMELESS

On Skid Row in Los Angeles, the Confirmation Classes of Leo Baeck Temple and All Saints Church supply the evening meal once a month at the Genesis Hotel, a single room occupancy facility (SRO) that the Temple and Church have rehabilitated.

At shelters operated by churches, synagogues, and mosques, you will frequently meet whole families or a group of friends who bring a meal regularly. I know a man who motivated half of his condo association to bring meals to a shelter.

You never know what a difference you can make.

A sage once explained that we should think of the world as hanging in the balance between good and evil. A single act on our part can tip the scales in either direction.

Your simple act of bringing a meal to the homeless shows that you care. By your example, others — like relatives, friends, and co-workers — may be inspired to do the same.

ORGANIZE A THRIFT SHOP 27

A thrift shop where second-hand items such as used clothing, shoes, toys, books, and/or appliances are sold is a good way to get your religious institution—and others in your community—involved in helping the poor and homeless.

Donations of merchandise are made by the congregation and other members of the community (usually through drives and/or by having a collection bin at the shop). Parishioners volunteer their services to operate the shop. To organize a thrift shop:

*Set up a committee within your congregation to manage the shop and coordinate volunteers;

*Find an area for the shop (at your religious center or other donated space);

*Decide which organizations will receive the funds and/or donated merchandise your shop generates;

*Determine the kind of merchandise you will carry (clothing, furniture, etc.) and seek donations;

*Ask for volunteers in your congregation or community to donate their time on a regular basis to run the shop, to sort through and display donations, to make deliveries and pick-ups.

If your religious center already has a thrift shop, you can help by becoming a volunteer and urging the shop to donate some of its proceeds to the homeless.

Some formerly homeless people have so much talent that they can make things which your organization, church, synagogue, or mosque can sell.

I once visited the Genesis Hotel, a single-room-occupancy facility on Los Angeles' Skid Row. That's where I met Raymond, a 47-year-old former draftsman from Houston who found himself nearly homeless in L.A.'s back alleys.

His room at the Genesis, filled with rocking horses, looked like a *toymaker's workshop — an ebony steed with an ivory yarn mane, a white stallion, and a cream-colored pony. He sold them for $175 or more as a donation for the Carlyle Center, the agency that had found him his room at the Genesis. He planned to use some of the proceeds to purchase power tools to accelerate the drilling and sanding of the horses. Two residents of Genesis have become his apprentices, and he hopes to leave a little business for his son.*

VOLUNTEER JOB TRAINING 28

Since 1988, Binding Together (BTI) has trained several hundred homeless men and women—each of whom has a history of substance abuse—to operate industrial capacity copying and binding machines. The trainees are referred from residential drug treatment centers and must be drug-free.

Funded in part by state and city agencies, BTI enlisted the support of corporations, which donated equipment, provided representatives for BTI's board and agreed to utilize BTI's copying services—and, most important, to hire its graduates. In it first year, BTI grossed over $250,000.

You can help by volunteering time and/or making donations to such organizations. Or suggest that your company set such a program in motion. If you are a small business owner, consider training a homeless person yourself or hiring graduates from programs such as BTI.

Bill Hodges, a Days Inn motel chain executive, became acquainted with homeless people at the Atlanta shelter where he volunteered. Feeling that the homeless could be trained as reservation clerks, he convinced Days Inn's CEO, Michael Leven, to visit the Atlanta shelter.

"When you get into a shelter and take a look at the homeless," said Leven, "(you realize that) they aren't dirty or falling off their feet drunk. They're everyday people who are down on their luck."

Leven was so impressed that he established a special program where the homeless receive social security cards and one-on-one computer training. Housing is provided at a local motel at $20 per day, with the company paying half. The clerks earn $5.50 an hour, receive health benefits, and have promotion opportunities. Since the program began, twenty people have maintained their positions, only a few have dropped out, and the turnover rate is less than that of other workers for Days Inn.

29 VOLUNTEER AT BATTERED WOMEN'S SHELTERS

Most battered women are involved in relationships with abusive husbands or other family members. Lacking resources and afraid of being found by their abusers, many may have no recourse other than a shelter or life on the streets once they leave home.

Fortunately, shelters designed especially for these women exist all over the country. In addition to providing safe haven, the shelters offer counseling and understanding. They work with local authorities on follow-up procedures to protect battered women and children from their abusers when they leave the shelter. Many women have children. Often they have no income. Many are poorly educated and have no work prospects. They need job training in addition to assistance in finding housing.

Volunteers handle shelter hotlines, pick up abused women and their children when they call, keep house, and offer counseling. Call your local shelter for battered women to see how you can help.

Fifty percent of all homeless women and children have found themselves in that situation as a result of domestic violence. If you know of such a person, encourage him or her to seek help.

Nearly every state has an 800 hot-line number for victims of domestic violence. The New Jersey number receives over 300 calls a month and, like many other states, offers service for the hearing impaired and provides bilingual assistance. To volunteer, call 800 information for the number and then offer your services for the hot-line, shelter assistance, or financial support.

V

Get Others Involved

TEACH ABOUT THE HOMELESS 30

If you do volunteer work with the homeless, you can become an enthusiast and extend your enthusiasm to others. How can you infect others with your own sense of devotion?

*By recognizing that your work with the homeless has not only educated you, it has empowered you to speak with authority.

*By writing letters to the editor and articles on the topic for local papers and by participating in paid advertising. All shape public opinions.

*By pressing housing issues at election time. Fund raising events present particularly effective moments for educating candidates, who have the power to promote affordable housing and other measures to help homeless people.

Here are some steps that volunteers in our shelter program have taken to educate others:

*Spoke at a religious service and at a Board of Trustees' meeting about their experiences working with the homeless.

*Duplicated cogent articles about homelessness from newspapers and magazines, and made them available on a table at the reception following religious services.

*Brought the subject of homelessness and poverty into the curriculum of our religious school.

*Asked the local principals to include the subject in the public school curriculum.

*Asked the presidents of the local service organizations (Kiwanis, Rotary, Soroptomists, etc.) to schedule a program on the homeless.

31 PUBLISH SHELTER INFORMATION

Despite all of our efforts to spread the word about shelters, it is surprising how many people — including the homeless themselves — are unaware of their own local shelters. Do you know where they are?

Well-run shelters are often not noticed by the community at large. A published listing of area shelters, food programs, and other assistance for the homeless can bring these programs to the attention of potential volunteers and donors of food, equipment, and money.

Contact your local newspapers, church or synagogue bulletins, or civic groups newsletters about the possibility of running a weekly or monthly listing of area services available to the homeless. This could include each organization's particular needs for volunteers, food, and other donations.

A poster is available for bookstores to use when displaying this book. The poster has space to fill in the locations of local shelters, food pantries, and clothing distribution centers. If your bookstore does not display the poster, ask them to do so.

Our local free food pantry ran precariously low on supplies during a long, bitterly cold winter a few years ago. They placed an article in the local paper requesting donations. The result: food flooded in.

The most common reaction was: "We had no idea that there was a food pantry in our town." And those who did know said that they just assumed there was plenty of food donated.

A single, brief newspaper notice changed the attitude of half the town.

ENLIST COMMUNITY ORGANIZATIONS AS ADVOCATES 32

Congress responds to voters. But homeless citizens rarely vote. And with a few exceptions, they don't visit or write their representatives. So if we don't speak up for them, who will?

By enlisting social justice organizations and entire memberships of synagogues and churches as advocates for the homeless, we can make Congress hear us just by our numbers.

To understand the potential number of advocates for the homeless in this nation, consider the Interfaith Hospitality Networks. Over 28,000 volunteers from hundreds of churches and synagogues in seven states are involved—all from just one modest-sized network!

Speak to your community's organizations. Enlist their voices in helping the homeless. Start a letter-writing campaign. Ask them to visit their state and federal representatives.

In January 1989 religious-sponsored social justice groups brought several hundred professional and volunteer activists to Washington, D.C. for a conference entitled, "Raising the Roof." Meeting at round tables with congresspeople, they discussed housing issues.

Most of the legislators had never before heard from religiously-motivated people who work the streets and shelters. Not only were they impressed by the step-by-step evaluation of housing legislation, but they also learned that many of their constituents care about this issue out of deep religious commitment. Since the conference, those advocates have lobbied, and when they did, they packed a bigger wallop than ever before. Every person who left that conference and reached out to his or her representative contributed to the passage of the landmark National Affordable Housing Act of 1990.

33 EDUCATE YOUR CHILDREN ABOUT THE HOMELESS

If we hope to aid the homeless, we must educate as many others about the situation as we can. And what better place to start than in our own home, with our own children?

Tell your children what you have learned about and help them to see the homeless as people. If you do volunteer work, take your sons and daughters along so they can meet with homeless people and see what can be done to help them. With older children, volunteer as a family in a soup kitchen or shelter. Suggest that they sort through the toys, books, and clothes they no longer use and donate them to shelters or organizations that assist the poor.

In my congregation, parents who serve meals at the shelter come with their children who play with the young guests. When they get home they discuss their experiences and feelings after those visits.

I also know parents who try to protect their children from ever seeing the homeless. That's a big mistake, for when the children do finally enter the real world, they will lack understanding. Children need to know very early that there is poverty and homelessness in their town, and that they can make a difference. This also enables our children to become more caring and sensitive human beings.

SIGN UP YOUR COMPANY/SCHOOL 34

Ask your company or school to host fund-raising events, such as raffles or craft sales, using co-workers or other students for volunteer assistance, and donate the proceeds to nonprofit organizations that aid the homeless.

You can also ask your company or school to match whatever funds you and your co-workers or friends can raise or are willing to donate for causes to help the homeless. (Be sure to have prepared concrete suggestions for how to raise funds, a specific list of organizations to donate them to, and exactly how funds are allocated.)

If you work for a large company or organization — or if your parents and friends do — approach the management to contribute to local or national charities. (See the back of this book for a list of organizations.) Often a "matching grant" works best — employers agree to donate (up to a certain limit) a dollar for every dollar any individual employee contributes.

Publishing companies donate their books each year to the Book Fair for the Homeless which benefits the Goddard-Riverside Community Center. The Center, on New York City's Upper West Side, provides day care, head start, and legal support for the poor and homeless.

On the weekend before a recent Book Fair, 20 dinners were held in private homes with contemporary writers in attendance including Roger Angell, Isaac Asimov, E. L. Doctorow, Gael Greene, Tom Wolfe, Erica Jong, and Kurt Vonnegut. During the week, performances by the Paperbag Players and bookreadings by the wife of the Mayor were held at schools. On Friday evening, there was a preview and live auction. The Book Fair itself took place on Saturday and Sunday. In its first five years, this event has raised half-a-million dollars for the needy and provided permanent homes for 500 people and assistance to thousands more.

35 RECRUIT LOCAL BUSINESSES

One of the easiest ways to involve local businesses is to organize food and/or clothing drives to aid organizations that reach the homeless. These are the steps involved:

*Contact your local shelters, food kitchens, synagogues, churches, or other organizations with programs to help the homeless and ask what types of food or clothing they need.

*Approach local grocery or clothing shops about setting up containers on their premises in which people can drop off donations. Give a time frame for the drive: a day, a weekend, a week. Remember, the longer the drive, the more arrangements needed for volunteer help, transportation, and storage.

*Ask the businesses to donate goods to the drive.

*Publicize the drive by placing announcements in local papers and on community bulletin boards and by posting signs and posters around your neighborhood. Be sure to list the specific types of goods you are seeking: nonperishable foods such as canned goods, and staples like flour, sugar, coffee; coats in good repair; clothing that is not too worn or stained, etc. Mention the organization to receive the donations and the businesses participating.

*Arrange for transportation of the donations. If you or other volunteers cannot do it, approach the designated shelter or organization to arrange for pickup or ask the local businesses if they can make a delivery.

❀

In my town, a party coordinator donated her talents to organize a "Thanksgiving Gathering" for people experiencing difficult times. As she put it, "Perhaps your family is far away...you've lost a spouse or loved one...or you're without work and having financial troubles."

Area merchants, especially restaurants, donated food and merchandise while the YMCA provided the space. Over 100 grateful guests enjoyed a happy Thanksgiving.

ASK YOUR CLERGY TO HELP 36

Among the various good works your clergy should be involved in are programs to help the homeless. Ask if they are aware of the problem in your community. If not, educate them about what you have learned—show them this book, for instance. Then ask them to get involved in community efforts to aid the homeless. Point out specific programs you may have uncovered. Suggest that the congregation become involved.

If your clergy are already active in this area, ask how you can assist them.

Six hundred churches and synagogues are involved in Interfaith Hospitality Networks in New Jersey, Ohio, Pennsylvania, Connecticut, Michigan, Minnesota, and Texas.

Here's how it works. Ten houses of worship take turns providing shelter and meals for homeless families. Each church and synagogue hosts for a week or two. They get plenty of guidance and hands-on support from a local network coordinating agency which provides transportation, counseling, and a comprehensive assistance program resulting in 70 percent of the families finding permanent housing.

Twenty-eight thousand volunteers are involved and the numbers grow every day. In one New Jersey county, the Network increased the number of shelter beds by 56 percent.

Contact National Interfaith Hospitality Networks for information and encouragement (908-273-1100).

37 SUGGEST YOUR CONGREGATION OFFER TITHES

If you regularly attend services at church, synagogue, or other religious organization, you might suggest to the congregation that everyone donate part of their regular offerings or tithe to a local organization that aids the homeless. Talk to religious officials about the idea; suggest that the congregation "adopt" a local charity and make regular donations of time, money, or supplies. Part of the Sunday collection or of the Yom Kippur appeal can be given to the "adopted" charity.

Whenever your synagogue, church, or mosque sponsors a breakfast, lunch, or dinner, add three percent to the cost of the event and direct those funds to agencies which help the homeless. You'll be surprised how quickly the dollars add up. And imagine if every house of worship participated! We'd be sponsoring affordable housing in every American city.

CREATE LISTS OF NEEDED DONATIONS 38

Most nonprofit organizations that aid the homeless can use donations of food, clothing, furniture, appliances, and other supplies. Often, they don't have the resources to make their needs widely known or to organize drives to bring donations in.

That's where you can help. And you don't need to leave your home; all you need is your phone. Call the organizations in your community that aid the homeless—the shelters, the halfway houses, the mobile food units, the food pantries, the relocation programs—and ask them what supplies they need on a regular basis. Make a list for each organization, along with its address, telephone number, and the name of a contact person.

Then mail these lists to community organizations that may wish to help with donations: religious centers (churches, synagogues, temples), associations (the American Legion, the Elks, the Knights of Columbus), local businesses, schools, and children's organizations such as Girl Scouts and Boy Scouts.

❊

On October 29, 1992 a truck arrived in southern New Jersey with thousands of blankets for the homeless. Since the 1960s, in churches across the country, collections have been taken on an annual "Blanket Sunday" to help Church World Service (the overseas relief agency of the National Council of Churches) provide blankets for starving people in Africa.

As the homeless population in the United States grew, more funds were raised so that blankets could also go to the needy in America. Reverend Lee Schmookler, director of the Goodwill Home and Mission in Newark, observed, "While blankets may seem token aid for a home-

less person, they are very definitely a need. Anything that helps the poor stretch a dollar is a benefit."

The Dayspring Center of Indianapolis, IN, runs a linens drive year around. The linens are given to guests to use while they reside at the shelter. When they obtain more permanent housing, they take the linens with them. Dayspring, which never buys linens, estimates that the linen donations are worth $25,000 a year.

VI

What Children Can Do

TEACH THEIR FRIENDS 39

Just as you can be an advocate for the homeless, so can your children. Ask them to tell their friends what you have taught them about helping the homeless. If your family does volunteer work, bring along some of your children's friends to watch. At school, your children can tailor school projects, such as book reports or speeches, around issues confronting the homeless. The more children learn about the hardships of the homeless, the more likely it is that they will pitch in to aid the poor and disadvantaged.

An eight-year-old girl was asked by her teacher to describe what it "might feel like to be homeless." Here is what she wrote:

"Well, time to go begging. Usually no one gives me anything, but it's worth a try anyway. Yesterday I didn't get anything because I was in a bad mood, yelling out all these bad words for no reason. See, no one understands that when you're homeless you have so many trapped emotions inside that you just explode."

Every school should dedicate a unit of curriculum to studying the homeless and developing a project on their behalf.

40 COLLECT TOYS AND GAMES FOR DONATION

Last year's toys are often forgotten toys. As children mature, they outgrow their dolls and trucks and games. Rather than having these items gather dust on a shelf or in a closet, ask your children to sort through the things they never play with and make a donation of the ones that are not too worn.

Once they have gone through their own toys, have them collect toys from friends and schoolmates. Then help the children find organizations that could make good use of toys and games, and take the items there with your children.

A chiropractor in Maryland offers health services at no charge if you donate toys, games, and food for the needy. In a large ad in the local newspaper, he offered his services on a particular Saturday and promised that the gifts would be distributed by his church to families throughout the county.

PREPARE FOOD AND GIFTS 41

Children's groups, like the Boy Scouts and the Brownies, are always looking for projects that will help needy people. Make a list of the food and gifts which young children and teens can make or collect to help the homeless. Then take that list to the teacher or group leader and discuss which ones would be appropriate for that age group and community. How about offering your services to help the children carry it through?

This is a great way to involve kids and to teach them about the needs of the homeless.

Here's a list of some of the groups you might approach:

Boy Scouts and Cub Scouts
Girl Scouts and Brownies
Play groups
Primary grades at public and private schools
Church and synagogue youth groups
Community centers
YMCA, YWCA, YMHA

Once a week, girls in a Brownie troop in Connecticut prepare dinner for 45 shelter guests.

Kindergarten children make placemats on holiday and seasonal themes and donate them to the local shelter. They brighten the meals and give people a feeling that everyone cares.

Boy Scouts of America have a nationwide project called "Scouting for Food." In communities across the country, hundreds of Cub Scouts, Explorers, and Boy Scouts, aided by their parents and other adult volunteers, distribute special contribution bags. They return later, collect the bags filled with staples, and distribute them to shelters and food pantries. The bags, contributed by a regional supermarket chain, list the items needed. Instructions include: "Place your filled bag on your doorstep by 9:00 a.m. the Saturday after you receive your bag. Scouts will pick up the bag no later than 3:00 p.m. (Please! No outdated items)."

Play groups in Minnesota and Massachusetts bake cupcakes and cookies and drop them off in the afternoon at shelters.

DONATE ADMISSION FEES FROM AN EVENT 42

Take advantage of some of the many events your children's school hosts during the year, such as plays, ball games, and dances. Ask your children to suggest to their teachers and school administrators that admission to one or more of these events be donated to a cause that helps the homeless. Or recommend that the admission charge be cans of food or clean blankets for donation to a shelter.

A church youth group in Michigan rented the high school auditorium and hired several rock groups to play. Since all proceeds would go to support the homeless, the Board of Education reduced the rental fee and the groups cut their charge by 50 percent.

The result: nearly a thousand people showed up and the teenagers donated $3,700 after expenses. That paid for two transitional apartments for the homeless for five months.

43 USE BIRTHDAY PARTIES TO HELP

Scavenger hunts are a favorite activity for a birthday party. Instead of asking the kids to find a red bow tie or a 1956 penny, try having them collect canned food for the homeless, the poor, and for unemployed people.

It's also a great project for a youth group at a church, synagogue, or community center.

The items can be bagged and taken to your local food pantry. Frequently, the stock at many food collection centers runs so low that they cannot supply the needs of those who come for help.

Here is the flyer that the youth of the First Baptist Church distributed door-to-door in Westfield, New Jersey. Parents drove cars with teams of five children each and then took the hundreds of cans they collected to the food pantry.

YOUTH IN ACTION

THE 5TH-10TH GRADE YOUTH

OF THE

FIRST BAPTIST CHURCH

OF WESTFIELD ARE CONDUCTING A

CANNED FOOD SCAVENGER HUNT

Would you please donate a few cans, jars,
or packages of food from your pantry?
Items will be delivered to the
Food Pantry of First Park Baptist Church,
Plainfield, for distribution to
the needy and unemployed.
Thank you!

CANNED GOODS SCAVENGER HUNT
TEAM #

ITEM	POINT	NO. COLL.	TOTAL	ITEM	POINT	NO. COLL.	TOTAL
Meat				Pears	5		
Tuna Fish	5			Pineapple	8		
Chicken	8			Mandarin Orang	8		
Sardine	10			Other Fruit	10		
Other Meat	10			Fruit Juice	10		
Veg.				**Miscellaneous**			
Soup	5			Nuts	10		
Creamed Soup	5			Reg. Coffee	5		
Other Soup	8			Decaf. Coffee	8		
Baked Beans	5			Flavored Coffee	10		
Whole Kernel Corn	5			Cocoa Mix	5		
Creamed Corn	8			Shortening	8		
Sweet Peas	5			Cereal	5		
Green Beans	5			Macaroni & Cheese	5		
Sweet Potatoes				Pasta - spaghetti			
or Yams	8			macaroni, etc.	5		
Whole Potatoes	5			spaghetti Sauce	8		
Sauerkraut	10			Peanut Butter	8		
Other Vegs.	8			Jelly	8		
				Granola Bars	10		
Fruit				Baby Food	5		
Apples	5						
Peaches	5						

44 PLAY WITH CHILDREN IN A SHELTER

Many children in shelters are cut off from others their own age. Shuffled from place to place, sometimes these kids don't attend school on a regular basis, and have no contact with other kids.

Bring a little joy to their lives by taking your children to a local shelter to play. Plan activities such as coloring, playing with dolls, or building model cars (take along whatever toys you'll need). Your own children will benefit, too.

I walked into our Temple's shelter early one evening. In one corner I saw a 15-year-old in my confirmation class playing checkers with a young guest. At a table, a 12-year-old girl was helping a pre-schooler choose different colored crayons for her sketch. Another Temple student was reading to a couple of kids. Their parents were there too, socializing with our adult guests and helping one woman fill out some forms.

When I see parents and children coming to the shelter together as a family to volunteer, I know that the guests gain a great deal and so does the volunteer family. The family feels that they really can live by their ideals and values and the guests know that people really care enough to take time for one-to-one contact.

VII

Really Make A Commitment

START A 45
SECOND HARVEST
PROGRAM

Second Harvest is a national food bank network of over 180 local food banks that supply shelters, soup kitchens, day care centers, senior programs, and other charities that serve meals. The food in this program is donated by restaurants, grocery stores, manufacturers, and distributors, among others. The network program typically arranges pickup and delivery of the donations.

If there isn't a program like this in place in your community already, this would be a good service to provide, both for local businesses that sell food (they get tax write-offs for donations and a chance to salvage perfectly good food rather than throwing it out) and for charities that provide meals to the homeless. Get in touch with Second Harvest to find out about starting a food recycling program in your community or supporting one already in your area.

Bill Liddell is an example of the difference one person can make through Second Harvest. A retired executive for a seed company, Liddell farms his three-quarter acre field in Mount Carmel, Connecticut and delivers the fresh produce free of charge to the Connecticut Food Bank, a Second Harvest agency. For four decades, he tilled the land, canning and freezing enough vegetables to supply his family of six throughout the winter. Now, through crop rotation and multiple plantings, Liddell harvests 40,000 pounds a year with the help of volunteers who work through October.

Liddell is just one of many suppliers, including Kellogg, Kraft, and McDonald's, that have provided over three billion pounds of food to distribute to the hungry.

16 EMPLOY THE HOMELESS

HELP WANTED
General Office Work. Welfare recipient, parolee,
ex-addict OK. Good salary, benefits. Will train.

That's the way Wildcat Service Corporation's Supported Work Program invites the "unemployable" to learn to work.

Best of all—the program works! More than half the people who sign on find permanent, well-paying jobs, often in maintenance, construction, clerical, or security work. Wildcat has placed homeless people with Manufacturers Hanover, the IRS, and the New York City Parks Department.

Many of the homeless want to work, but lack the opportunity. Some are unskilled, others aren't. All are looking for a chance. Whether you use a homeless training program such as Wildcat to hire someone, or employ a person in your business through a shelter, you both benefit. Remember, 25 percent of the people in shelters do work part or full time and most of those who don't are willing and able to.

Ego Brown decided that instead of offering a handout every time he passed a homeless person in downtown Washington, D.C., he would employ them for his outdoor shoeshine business. They would pull themselves up by other people's bootstraps.

His recruits were given a shower, a tuxedo, and a portable stand. His "program" proved successful, and in the summer of 1985, a municipal social worker started referring homeless people to him.

A member of my congregation shared some of my writings on the homeless with his co-workers at a local plastics company. After discussing ways to help, they decided to send the firm's van to our synagogue's shelter and invite guests to return to the company for employment interviews. It gave the guests valuable experience interviewing and opened up several job prospects.

HELP THE HOMELESS 47
APPLY FOR AID

Governmental aid is available for homeless people, but many may not know where to find it or how to apply. Since they don't have a mailing address, governmental agencies may not be able to reach them.

You can help by directing the homeless to intermediaries, such as shelters or organizations like Catholic Charities, that let them know what aid is available and help them to apply for it. If you want to be an advocate or intermediary for the homeless yourself, you can contact these organizations as well.

Often what is needed is a combination of a homeless person who wants to be helped and an individual who cares enough to get involved and persevere. That combination produces incredible results. It explodes the tired stereotype that homeless people do not want to be helped. And it proves that every one of us can make a difference.

When illness forced Albert Bishop to leave his job as a security guard in 1984, he became homeless. He missed the deadline to apply for public and subsidized housing because he was in the hospital.

Once released, Bishop lived with a friend whom he later found was on crack. Meanwhile, he sought help from every agency he could find, visited projects, and wrote his congressman. As the situation grew worse at his friend's apartment, he decided to put his entire medical and housing history down on paper.

Then he brought that history to Catholic Charities, where Ruth Francis, a caseworker, became his advocate. Over the course of eight months, she helped him track down subsidized housing. By insisting that the agencies respond to her, she kept the process going.

In September 1989, Bishop moved into a City Housing Authority three-room apartment in Harlem. It was, he said, "the hide-away I always dreamed of." Without Ruth Francis' dogged determination, he would probably still be homeless.

48 STAND UP FOR THE CIVIL RIGHTS OF THE HOMELESS

We don't often realize that the homeless citizens of America have the same civil rights as the rest of us.

In recent elections for example, volunteers at shelters and elsewhere helped homeless people register to vote . . . even though they had "no fixed address" at the moment. Some officials would not permit citizens without a permanent address to vote. Again and again attorneys were required to go to court to defend the right to vote.

Local Board of Elections officials in Orange County (NY) attempted to deny homeless men the right to vote in the 1992 Presidential election, maintaining that they were transients. The Coalition for the Homeless led a campaign to win the vote for them. One day before the election, Judge Louis A. Barone invited the men to his courtroom, called them one-by-one and granted them their right to vote. "It's good to see you all here," he observed. "You should all be congratulated for going out of your way to vote."

✳

In New York City and elsewhere the American Civil Liberties Union and others have fought for the right of homeless people to beg. There are numerous other examples — recently in Miami supporters of the homeless pressured to establish "safe zones" where homeless people could go and receive protection from those who were stealing from them, or otherwise maltreating them. In fact, one of the purposes was to protect them from the police, who often used violence to remove homeless people from the streets.

VIII

Help To
End Homelessness

JOIN HABITAT FOR HUMANITY 49

Habitat for Humanity, a Christian housing ministry, builds houses for families in danger of becoming homeless. Volunteers from the community and Habitat homeowners erect the houses. Funding is through donations from churches, corporations, foundations, and individuals.

The community chapters of Habitat, acting as banks, hold no-interest loans on the houses built. As families make monthly payments, the funds are recycled for the next home built. Typical payback on a loan is $150 a month, manageable even on a very low income. The average cost to a family for their Habitat home in the United States is $30,000, plus 500 hours of "sweat equity"—their own physical labor and their commitment to help construct other homes.

Anyone can volunteer to help on a Habitat project. Since leaving office, Former President Jimmy Carter and his wife Rosalyn have spent one week every summer working on a Habitat project, one of over 10,000 dwellings built or rehabilitated worldwide since 1990. By having needy and affluent people work together in equal partnership, Habitat not only erects houses, but also builds new relationships and a sense of community.

Contact your local Habitat for Humanity or write Habitat's national office.

Catherine Martinez shed tears of joy as she thanked the men and women with the Santa Fe, New Mexico, Habitat for Humanity who had come to help build a home for herself, her husband, and their six children, ages five through eighteen. The family, along with Catherine's parents, lived in an 800-square foot trailer. Their living

conditions had become intolerable, putting them at great risk of becoming homeless.

Catherine's husband, Robert, a Vietnam vet suffering from post-traumatic syndrome, receives $19,000 a year in disability benefits, placing them below the poverty level for a family of their size.

"I'm overcome with emotion," said Catherine. "The going was rough, but my faith in God carried me through. There's nothing better than to give of yourself to others." Then she gestured to a woman who lived in the home that the Santa Fe Habitat had just completed. "Joan's here today, building my house—and I'll be at the next one that Habitat builds."

FORM A 50
TRANSITIONAL
HOUSING PROGRAM

One of the most potent homeless-prevention services a community can offer residents who are in danger of eviction is a transitional housing program.

These programs help people hang on to their current residences or assist them in finding more affordable ones. The methods include steering people to appropriate social service and community agencies, helping them move out of shelters, and providing funds for rent, mortgage payments, and utilities.

One such program is the Elim Transitional Housing program, founded by Sue Watlov Phillips in 1983 in Minneapolis. Starting as a shelter at the Elim Baptist Church, it evolved, with the help of the local utility, North States Power, into a transitional housing program which has benefited over 6,000 people.

Elim's success is being duplicated across the nation by hundreds of community-based groups. Any city or suburban cluster of 50,000 or more people either has such a group or has the potential to create it.

For information on transitional housing programs, contact the Homelessness Information Exchange.

Until Jeanette Veldhouse-Sellier's twenty-two-year marriage ended in divorce, she never imagined that her middle-class family would ever be on the verge of homelessness. How did it happen? Her husband walked out of their Minneapolis home, leaving her with two children, thirteen and eighteen. He promptly lost his job, which meant that alimony and child support ceased.

Jeanette, who has a degree in child psychology, lost her well-paying *position as director of a learning center. The best work she could find was at $5 an hour.*

Once she exhausted her meager savings, she fell behind in her mortgage payments even with help from her mother. She was within ten days of eviction when she sought help from the Elim Transitional Housing program. It put her in touch with the county assistance office, which provided her with a security deposit for an apartment. Elim covered part of the first six months' rent. The program also directed her to food banks for groceries, a medical clinic, and a fuel assistance agency that helped with oil bills.

Jeanette—who was within days of being homeless—is today the administrator of a youth program. "You think of the stereotypical homeless person as someone of low income who doesn't have an education and who's probably anti-social," Jeanette says. "But we're a middle-class American family. Without Elim's help, we'd have had to live on the streets."

WRITE TO ORGANIZATIONS 51

Some of the largest corporations in America have joined the battle for low-income housing. Through the use of the tax credit or by outright grants, they are participating with federal and state government, not-for-profit and community-based groups to build desperately needed housing in Chicago, Cleveland, Los Angeles, Philadelphia, and dozens of other cities.

If a company invests $1 million in a financing pool for low-income housing, over the course of fifteen years it could realize $2.3 million in tax savings. How does it work? The federal government assigns tax credits to each state. The state housing authority then passes these tax credits on to private developers and investors who build low-cost housing.

Foundations and religious groups are also critically needed partners in this effort.

*Write major corporations, foundations, and religious groups urging them to join the effort.

*Thank them if they are already partners in a major program and ask them to do even more. You'll be surprised. A few letters to people at the top will go a long way . . .

In 1973, members of the Church of the Savior in Washington, D.C., approached businessman James Rouse for help in funding the restorations of run-down apartment buildings. At first he suggested they try governmental programs instead. But they persisted. Impressed by their dedication, he agreed to put up the $625,000 they needed. With 50,000 hours of volunteer labor from the community, the church was able to rehabilitate the buildings.

Their success led Rouse in the 1980s to establish the Enterprise

Foundation, a non-profit organization that links developers and investors for low-income housing projects.

Corporations help in other ways:

The Nehemiah Plan began in East Brooklyn when five pastors from Roman Catholic, Baptist, and Lutheran churches created a coalition of 52 local organizations with more than 30,000 members. Their purpose: to build housing for low and moderate income families. The result: local banks and corporations joined the effort which produced thousands of attached houses and apartments. And they are still going strong.

A similar story in North Philadelphia, which looked like a war zone in 1968. That transformation—with new solar townhouses and hundreds of renovated units—was sparked by the National Temple Baptist Church and the non-profit corporation they created. Their partners? American Express, the Catholic Church, The Ford Foundation, Pew Trust, Mellon Bank, and the Local Initiatives Support Corporation.

CONTACT YOUR GOVERNMENT REPRESENTATIVES 52

Our legislators rarely receive more than three visits or ten letters about any subject. When the numbers exceed that amount, they sit up and take note. Personal visits are the most potent. Letters are next; telephone calls are third best.

Housing issues don't come up that often, so your public officials will listen, particularly if you write as a constituent who is not a housing advocate whose job depends on increased funding or a tenant trying to hold on to an apartment. So let your government representatives know that you're concerned about housing and are willing to support decent programs to help the homeless, such as those promoting affordable housing, job training, health care, inner-city education, and support services. And keep letting your legislators know that your vote may be decided by their stand on those issues.

Jerald Scott, who oversees human welfare issues for the United Methodist Church, put it bluntly: "We must tell our representatives that if they do not make low-income housing their priority, we are not going to send them back to Washington."

A congregation in Mississippi organized a letter-writing campaign on behalf of affordable housing legislation. A few weeks later, the administrative assistant of the local U.S. Congressman called the pastor to tell him that his office was "overwhelmed" by the concern expressed by his congregants. The pastor was gratified, but also curious. So he asked the aide how many letters were received. The answer: "Four or five." Your 29-cent stamp goes a long way!

53 PUSH FOR STATE HOMELESSNESS PREVENTION PROGRAMS

While states routinely supply aid for the poor and homeless, many do not have programs to prevent homelessness. Generally, these programs provide funds and other services to those who will lose their homes in the immediate future unless something is done. Homelessness comes at great financial and human cost to the families who are evicted or foreclosed. Also, prevention saves money for taxpayers—as well as the heartache for those who face losing their homes.

What does it take for a state to have an effective, low-cost homelessness prevention program? It takes enlightened advocates and a few thousand people in and out of government who are convinced that homelessness is a problem that can be solved.

The men and women who create, promote, and support programs to help the homeless are average citizens, like you and me. The people who establish shelters in churches and synagogues and centers for "hopelessness prevention" are the ones we sit next to on Friday nights or Sunday mornings. There are no miracles here. Only concern for others.

The state of New Jersey has one of the best homelessness prevention programs in the nation. Its purpose: to provide "temporary assistance of last resort (loans, security, etc.) to households facing imminent eviction or foreclosure, because for reasons beyond their control they lack funds." The urgent need might be the result of a medical crisis, a natural disaster, nonpayment of child support, job loss, or a delay in receiving government benefits.

SEND US YOUR IDEAS 54

Each of the creative and successful ways to help the homeless described in this book reaches a fraction of the homeless. But one by one, each effort added together will eventually transform our cities, suburbs, and rural communities into a society we can be proud of, where food and shelter is something everyone can take for granted.

Be creative—develop your own ideas for helping the homeless and send them to us. We'll spread the good word to others.

Send your ideas to:

54 WAYS YOU CAN HELP THE HOMELESS
P.O. Box 712
Westfield, N.J. 07091

Resources

American Affordable Housing Institute
P.O. Box 118
New Brunswick, NJ 08903

California Coalition for the Homeless
1010 S. Flower Street
Los Angeles, CA
213-746-7677

Church & Temple Housing
502 1/2 S. Main Street
Los Angeles, CA 90013
213-627-3832

Coalition for the Homeless
500 Eighth Avenue
New York, NY 10018
212-695-8700

Common Cents New York, Inc.
500 Eighth Avenue
New York, NY 10018
212-736-6437

Community for Creative Non-Violence
425 Second Street, NW
Washington, D.C. 20001
202-393-4409

Community Workshop on Economic Development
100 S. Morgan Street
Chicago, IL 60607

Dayspring Center
1537 N. Central
Indianapolis, IN 46202
317-635-6785

Enterprise Foundation
505 American City Building
Columbia, MD 21044
301-964-1230

The Ford Foundation
320 East 43 Street
New York, NY 10017

Friends Committee on National Legislation
245 Second Street., NE
Washington, D.C. 20002-5795

Goddard-Riverside Community Center
593 Columbus Avenue
New York, NY 10024
212-873-6600

Habitat for Humanity
121 Habitat Street
Americus, GA 31709-3498
912-924-6935

Homelessness Information Exchange
1830 Connecticut Avenue
Washington, DC 20009
202-462-7551

House Pins, Inc.
80 Second Street
South Portland, ME 04106
207-799-6116

IMPACT
110 Maryland Avenue, NE
Washington, D.C. 20002
202-544-8636

Interfaith Coalition for Housing
United Methodist Church
100 Maryland Avenue, NE
Washington, D.C. 20002
202-488-5653

Interfaith Council for the Homeless of Union County
724 Park Avenue
Plainfield, NJ 07060
908-753-4001

The Interfaith Nutrition Network
148 Front Street
Hempstead, NY 11550
516-486-8506

Legal Action Center for the Homeless
220 E. 44th Street
New York, NY 10009
212-529-4240

Local Initiatives Support Corporation
733 Third Avenue, Eighth Floor
New York, NY 10017
212-529-4240